CW01501709

Original title:

Silken Branches Under the Faerie Shelf

Copyright © 2025 Swan Charm

Author: Daisy Dewi

ISBN HARDBACK: 978-1-80559-404-8

ISBN PAPERBACK: 978-1-80559-903-6

The Breath of Nature's Guardian

In whispers soft, the trees stand tall,
Guardians of secrets, they shelter all.
Leaves dance gently in the evening light,
Breath of nature, pure and bright.

Mountains echo with a timeless song,
Their mighty peaks where the spirits belong.
Rivers flow with stories untold,
In their depths, mysteries unfold.

The skies embrace a canvas wide,
Clouds drift slowly, like dreams they bide.
Stars awaken in the velvet night,
Nature's wonders, a soothing sight.

Wildflowers bloom in fields of gold,
Colors vibrant, a sight to behold.
Bees hum softly, gathering sweet,
Harmony found where nature meets.

As twilight descends, shadows grow long,
The guardian breathes, a soft, sweet song.
In every rustle, every sigh,
Nature's spirit whispers, never die.

Soft Threads of Magic Among the Boughs

In the quiet of dusk, whispers flow,
Soft threads of magic, gently aglow.
The leaves dance lightly, a sweet ballet,
As twilight's charm invites the day.

Winds carry secrets, old and wise,
Underneath the vast and starry skies.
Branches entwine in a tender embrace,
Holding the dreams of this sacred space.

Soft murmurs echo, stories unseen,
Where shadows linger, and wonders convene.
A heartbeat of nature, a lullaby sweet,
In the forest's arms, all lost souls meet.

The ground is woven with emerald thread,
Paths of enchantment, where few have tread.
Time stretches thin, like fog in the morn,
In this realm of magic, dreams are reborn.

With every step, the heart draws near,
To the pulse of the woods, so vibrant and clear.
In soft threads of magic, we find our way,
Among the boughs, forever we'll stay.

Lullabies of the Elderwood

Beneath the arches of the ancient trees,
Whispers of lullabies dance in the breeze.
Each note a caress, soft as the night,
Weaving together the shadows and light.

Crickets sing sweetly, a rhythmic refrain,
While fireflies flicker like stars in the rain.
Each melody carries a story untold,
Of spirits and magic, both timid and bold.

A hush falls gently, the world settles down,
Wrapped in a blanket of deep, calming sound.
The moon hangs low, a watchful eye,
Over the slumbering dreams drifting by.

In the heart of the Elderwood, peace takes flight,
Where wishes are whispered to the cloak of night.
Every echo is woven with love and care,
Each lullaby lingers, rich as the air.

So close your eyes tight, let your worries unwind,
In the cradle of verdure, solace you'll find.
With the lullabies sung by the leaves so old,
Drift into slumber, be gentle, be bold.

Echoes of Dreamweavers

In dawn's early light, the dreamweavers sigh,
Painting the skies where the memories lie.
Each thread of their art, a glimpse of the past,
Spinning together the shadows they cast.

Whispers of dreams in the cool morning haze,
Echo through valleys, their sweet, silver praise.
With each breath, stories begin to unfurl,
Like petals of twilight in a soft, gentle whirl.

They dance on the edges of waking and sleep,
Where secrets are hidden, and silence runs deep.
Upon woven winds, their fables take flight,
Guided by starlight, in the depth of the night.

The tapestry glimmers, capturing light,
Echoes of laughter and moments of fright.
Each whisper, a promise, a tale to be spun,
In the realm of the dreamers, all hearts beat as one.

With every new dawn, their magic renews,
Woven in joy, and sometimes in blues.
So heed the soft whispers, let your spirit roam,
In the echoes of dreamweavers, always find home.

Beneath the Enchanted Arbor

Beneath the arbor where moonlight weaves,
Secrets lie dormant among whispering leaves.
A canopy drapes in a silvery hue,
Guarding the dreams of the night's quiet view.

With roots that entwine in the earth's gentle hold,
Stories of magic and moments of old.
In shadows that linger, the air's thick with lore,
Each breath an adventure, a key to the door.

Branches stretch wide, like arms welcoming near,
Inviting the wanderers, sharing their cheer.
A carpet of petals, soft underfoot,
Guides weary souls as their journeys bear fruit.

In this sacred haven, time whispers along,
Where echoes of laughter cradle our song.
Underneath stars, in the heart of the night,
We gather our hopes, fueled by love's warm light.

So linger a while where the spirits convene,
Beneath the enchanted, where all is serene.
In nature's embrace, let your worries subside,
For here in the arbor, pure magic abides.

A Dance of Light and Nature's Caress

In morning's glow, the petals sigh,
As golden rays kiss earth and sky.
A gentle breeze brings whispers soft,
Where life awakens, dreams drift aloft.

Among the trees, shadows sway low,
Dancing light in a vibrant show.
Leaves shimmer bright in a fleeting glance,
Nature inviting, a wondrous dance.

Rivers hum with a lulling tune,
Reflecting hues of the bright, warm moon.
Florals bloom in a colorful spree,
Nature's canvas, wild and free.

The mountains stand with majesty tall,
Guardians of whispers, a timeless call.
Through valleys deep, the echoes play,
In harmony, love finds its way.

So, let us swirl in this sacred place,
Embracing the magic, the grand embrace.
For in this moment, hearts align,
A dance of light, where souls entwine.

The Faery's Gaze Through Dewy Veils

In twilight's mist, the faery glows,
With sparkling wings, where mystery flows.
Through dewy veils, she flits and glides,
In moonlight's embrace, her spirit abides.

Amongst the blooms, whispers entwine,
A call to magic, a fate divine.
Soft, gentle laughter fills the air,
A symphony woven with utmost care.

Her eyes hold secrets of ages past,
In twilight dances, the shadows cast.
Each twinkle a tale, each flutter a dream,
In the world's heartbeat, she stirs the stream.

Around her, starlight begins to weave,
In a tapestry spun, where shadows believe.
The earth blossoms forth with colors anew,
In the faery's gaze, all wonders accrue.

So hush your heart, let dreams take flight,
In the dewy veils of the soft night.
For the faery waits with a gentle grace,
Guiding us all to a sacred space.

Enigma of the Veiled Canopy

Beneath the boughs where shadows dance,
An enigma whispers, igniting chance.
Secrets linger in the rustling leaves,
A timeless tale, the forest weaves.

Filtered light paints a canvas lush,
In dappled patterns, the heartbeats hush.
Every rustle a promise, each sigh a clue,
The veil of nature, so ancient and true.

Roots intertwine like stories untold,
In the earth's embrace, the past unfolds.
Mystery deepens with every stride,
In the canopy's heart, wonders reside.

Dance with the shadows, sing with the breeze,
Unlocking the whispers among the trees.
For in this realm of the veiled unknown,
The spirit of nature is vividly shown.

So wander softly through nature's grace,
Embrace the enigma, the open space.
For in the whispers of the quiet night,
Lies the magic, the hidden light.

Crystals Nestled in Bramble's Heart

In tangled thorns, where shadows lie,
Crystals glisten, catching the eye.
Nestled softly in nature's keep,
Hidden treasures where secrets sleep.

Sunlight glows through emerald leaves,
Whispers of wonder, the heart believes.
Each gem a story, a fragment lost,
In bramble's heart, the beauty embossed.

Wild roses bloom with fragrant sighs,
As nature's gems catch the bright skies.
With every petal, a tale unfolds,
In a moment of magic, the world beholds.

So tread with care, the path is rare,
In the bramble's heart, find jewels laid bare.
With every step, let your spirit soar,
For in this wonder, there's always more.

Crystals twinkling with a soft embrace,
A dance of nature in exquisite grace.
In bramble's heart, life's secrets abide,
Inviting us all to take the ride.

Tranquil Murmurs of the Sylvan Realm

In quiet woods where shadows play,
The whispers of the trees convey,
Soft breezes brush the leaves so light,
A symphony of peace at night.

Beneath the stars, the rivers flow,
A mirror for the moon's soft glow.
Each ripple tells a tale untold,
Of ancient dreams and secrets old.

The gentle rustle stirs the mind,
In nature's arms, true solace find.
The crickets chirp a lullaby,
As time unfolds a breeze's sigh.

A path where wildflowers bloom bright,
Invites the wanderer each night.
Here in this realm, hearts learn to mend,
As nature's songs begin to blend.

The tranquil murmurs of the glade,
Compose a song that will not fade.
In sylvan realms, we lose and gain,
A harmony we can't restrain.

Secrets of the Enchanted Thicket

Deep in the thicket, shadows twine,
Whispers of magic, frame the vine.
The secrets dwell in earthy mounds,
Where ancient wisdom softly bounds.

Gentle creatures roam the night,
Glimmers of hope in fading light.
Each rustle tells of dreams long past,
In the thicket's hold, we breathe at last.

Moonbeams dance on leaves so green,
Invisible paths are often seen.
Echoes of laughter fill the air,
In the thicket's heart, joys are rare.

Petals of midnight softly gleam,
Guardians of every hidden dream.
With each step, the thicket sways,
Revealing secrets in quiet ways.

Beneath the stars, let worries cease,
In enchanted thickets, find your peace.
The secrets here forever grow,
In whispered tales and steady flow.

The Folklore of Wistful Whimsy

In realms of whimsy, stories bloom,
Where laughter hides and dreams consume.
Folklore weaves through every sigh,
In the heart of youth, it will not die.

Giggles echo in sunlit glades,
Where shadows dance in playful parades.
A tapestry of joy is spun,
In wistful whispers, hearts are won.

With every tale, the spirits rise,
Imagination soars in the skies.
The lore of old caresses the soul,
Freed by the magic that makes us whole.

In every corner, a smile awaits,
For whimsy thrives where love creates.
A sprinkle of laughter and a dash of cheer,
In the folklore's embrace, we have no fear.

So gather 'round, let stories flow,
In whimsy's dance, time moves slow.
The tales of wonder forever gleam,
A cherished gift, life's sweetest dream.

In the Embrace of Nature's Caress

Upon the hill, where wildflowers sway,
Nature's arms cradle night and day.
The scent of earth and pine entwined,
In the embrace, pure peace we find.

With every breath, the forest sings,
Of hidden joys that nature brings.
Gentle streams hum a lullaby,
In nature's hold, worries drift by.

The mountains stand like guardians bold,
While ancient tales of life unfold.
Skyward birds in graceful flight,
Guide the heart towards the light.

With every path beneath the sun,
An adventure waits for everyone.
In meadows green, souls intertwine,
In the caress of nature, we shine.

Through rustling leaves and starlit skies,
Moments of magic softly arise.
In nature's arms, we are complete,
The world in essence, pure and sweet.

Lullabies Beneath the Verdant Sphere

In the hush of twilight's breath,
Whispers dance on leaves anew,
Crickets hum their softest song,
As dreams take flight beneath the blue.

Moonlit shadows weave and sway,
Beneath the canopy so wide,
Nature cradles weary hearts,
In her arms, we bide our time.

Stars like embers softly glow,
Guiding the night's gentle glide,
Each lullaby a tender thread,
Stitched in warmth, where love resides.

The breeze brings tales from afar,
Of worlds unseen and dreams unfurled,
In this realm of velvet hues,
A symphony of night is twirled.

Close your eyes, let worries part,
As the earth wraps you in peace,
In the cradle of nature's heart,
Find the solace that will never cease.

Chronicles of the Glimmering Thicket

In the thicket's secret shade,
Stories linger, softly spun,
Whispers of the wildwood breath,
Carried lightly, one by one.

Leafy tomes of ages past,
Hold the echoes of the trees,
In their gaze, the spirits play,
Weaving myths within the breeze.

Through the bramble, trails unfold,
Footprints etched on mossy ground,
Each step reveals a tale untold,
In this haven, magic's found.

Sunbeams filter, casting gold,
On the canvas of the leaves,
Nature's heart is brave and bold,
In her lore, the spirit weaves.

Hear the silence, soft and clear,
Awakening the dreams we bear,
In the thicket, time stands still,
With each moment, breathe the air.

Threads of Dawn in Secret Nooks

Morning breaks with silent grace,
In the nooks where shadows rest,
Gentle whispers stir the air,
A tender touch, a newfound quest.

Sunlight filters, warm and pure,
Kissing petals, life ignites,
In the dew, a world reborn,
Promising enchantment in heights.

Birdsong weaves a vibrant thread,
Through the tapestry of day,
Each note a spark, a wish, a hope,
As the night drifts far away.

In quiet corners, dreams arise,
Bathed in light of soft embrace,
Every moment, fresh and bright,
In secret nooks, find your place.

Follow the dawn, it leads you near,
To the heart of what's begun,
In the stillness, breathe in deep,
Threads of light where shadows run.

The Enchantment of Living Silk

In the garden where secrets dwell,
Petals pulse with soft allure,
Threads of silk, a tale to tell,
Of nature's art, so pure, so sure.

Gentle breezes weave their dance,
Caressing blossoms, bright and fine,
Every shimmer holds a chance,
To unfold in the sun's design.

Colors blend in vibrant shades,
As the world becomes alive,
In this realm where beauty fades,
Yet, somehow always will survive.

Listen closely, hear their song,
Nature's whispers soft and sweet,
In this place where hearts belong,
Find the magic beneath your feet.

Veils of wonder, draped in light,
Spinning dreams from dusk till dawn,
In this silk, find pure delight,
As the night kisses the morn.

Whispers of the Starlit Grove

In the grove where shadows play,
Stars above begin to sway.
Softly murmurs drift through trees,
Caught in night's gentle breeze.

Moonlight spills on emerald ground,
Magic whispers all around.
Creatures stir beneath the light,
Hiding secrets of the night.

Branches sway with quiet grace,
Nature's peace, a soft embrace.
Every rustle, every sound,
Echoes deep from underground.

In the stillness, hearts take flight,
Lost in dreams that feel so right.
Under stars, our worries fade,
In this grove, our paths are laid.

Listen close, the night does sing,
To the magic dreams can bring.
Close your eyes and drift away,
In the grove, forever stay.

Veils of Enchantment in the Moonlight

Veils of mist in silver hue,
Whisper secrets old and new.
Moonlight dances on the stream,
Weaving threads of twilight dream.

Beneath the sky, the world ignites,
Filling hearts with wondrous sights.
Every leaf a story tells,
In the night where magic dwells.

Stars align, a cosmic dance,
In their glow, we find romance.
Veils of dreams, so soft, so bright,
Wrap us in their gentle light.

In this realm of mystic grace,
Every whisper finds its place.
Time stands still, lost in the night,
Chasing shadows, pure delight.

As the moon begins to wane,
Keep this magic, hold the reign.
Through the veils we wander far,
Guided by a single star.

Secrets Hidden in the Twilight Canopy

In the twilight's soft embrace,
Secrets hide without a trace.
Leaves murmur tales with the breeze,
Echoes wrapped in ancient trees.

Beneath the canopy so vast,
Whispers of the future, past.
Flickers of a dawn to come,
Breathless silence, hearts go numb.

Colors fade to shades of gray,
In the hush, we long to stay.
Every rustle, every sigh,
Tells a story, oh so shy.

As the sun dips down to sleep,
Twilight guards the dreams we keep.
In its arms, we find our peace,
In this moment, time's release.

Listen close, the night unfolds,
Secrets wrapped in threads of gold.
Underneath the stars that gleam,
We embrace the deepest dream.

Dance of the Ethereal Leaves

Ethereal leaves in the air,
Whirling softly, without care.
In their dance, the world dissolves,
Mysteries the heart resolves.

Golden hues in fading light,
Every leaf a tale of flight.
Windswept whispers, spirits soar,
Nature calls us to explore.

Falling softly to the ground,
In their rustle, joy is found.
In this dance of earth and sky,
Every heartbeat, a sigh.

Twisted branches, shadows play,
Guide our steps along the way.
Moonlit paths before us gleam,
In this space, we drift and dream.

Together, we will dance anew,
In the twilight's gentle view.
Every movement feels so free,
In the dance of memory.

Journeys Through Arcadian Passages

In quiet woods where shadows play,
The winding paths lead hearts astray.
With whispered tales, the leaves confide,
In secrets hidden, dreams abide.

Upon the stream, the sunlight gleams,
Reflecting hopes, entwined in dreams.
With every step, the spirit soars,
In Arcadia, love restores.

Through fragrant blooms and gentle sighs,
The world unfolds beneath the skies.
Each journey taken, paths unplanned,
Reveal the magic of the land.

Beneath the arch of ancient trees,
The essence of time drifts with ease.
In every turn, a charm awaits,
For life is woven with such fates.

The evening stars light up the night,
Guiding lost souls with their light.
In journeys, bonds are formed anew,
Through Arcadian passages, we pursue.

Memory's Tapestry Among the Arbors

Beneath the branches, memories dwell,
In whispers soft like a gentle bell.
Each leaf a story, each breeze a song,
In the arbors where we belong.

The sunlit hours, like threads entwined,
We weave our dreams, with love aligned.
Moments captured, both bright and small,
In the tapestry, we recall.

Time flows gently like a stream,
Carrying echoes of a dream.
In corners shaded, laughter rings,
As memory's dance through the heart sings.

With every visit, the past awakes,
A symphony of the joy it makes.
Among the arbors, we take our stand,
Embracing the warmth of the land.

In twilight's glow, our spirits merge,
With every pulse, our hearts they surge.
In memory's tapestry, we find,
The timeless threads of love entwined.

A Sojourn in the Enchanted Wilds

In forests deep, where fairies dwell,
A sojourn calls, with magic to tell.
Among the ferns and ancient trees,
Whispers float upon the breeze.

The hidden streams, with laughter flow,
Where secrets bloom and wildflowers grow.
In every shadow, a story lives,
In enchanted wilds, the heart forgives.

With every rustle, the world unfolds,
An adventure born as twilight enfolds.
The call of night, the moonlight's grace,
In nature's arms, we find our place.

Through glades adorned with starlit hues,
We wander far, the path we choose.
In every sigh, a promise made,
A sojourn sweet that will not fade.

As dawn approaches, colors blend,
In enchanted wilds, the journey ends.
Yet in our hearts, the magic stays,
To light our dreams in endless ways.

Locations of Forgotten Dreams

In dusty corners, shadows hide,
Locations lost where dreams abide.
With each step, the echoes call,
Of whispered hopes that softly fall.

Beneath the weight of time's embrace,
We seek the past in a hidden place.
A tapestry woven with glimmers bright,
Of forgotten dreams that dance in light.

Through crumbling walls and faded halls,
The laughter soft, the silence falls.
In these still moments, we find our grace,
In locations where time's lost face.

Each step taken, a journey reborn,
In the heart's garden, new dreams are worn.
With courage steeped in memories true,
We fashion the future from what we view.

In the silence deep and shadows long,
We gather strength, we chant our song.
For in these places, our spirits gleam,
And breathe again life into dreams.

A Canopy of Celestial Serenades

Beneath the stars, the night unfolds,
A melody of dreams retold,
Each twinkle sings a tale so bright,
In harmony, the dark meets light.

The moonbeams cast a silver glow,
On secret paths where stardust flows,
With whispers soft, the shadows play,
In cosmic dance, they drift away.

Galaxies in the velvet sky,
A symphony that breathes a sigh,
They weave a tapestry of hope,
On angel wings, we learn to float.

In gentle tones the night reveals,
The universe, its heart, it feels,
With every sound, the silence sings,
A cosmic lullaby takes wing.

So lay your burdens, close your eyes,
Let celestial serenades arise,
In this embrace, the night will weave,
A timeless peace, we dare believe.

The Sprightly Dance at Dusk

As daylight dims, the colors play,
In shades of gold, they drift away,
With every leap, the shadows spin,
A sprightly dance, where dreams begin.

The breeze arrives with soft embrace,
Whispers of night, they gently trace,
While fireflies twinkle in delight,
Their lanterns glowing, a welcome sight.

On pathways framed by fading light,
The world transforms, a wondrous sight,
With each footfall, the heart takes chance,
To lose itself in twilight's dance.

The stars peek out from velvet skies,
As dusk adorns with lullabies,
Each step a rhythm of the heart,
In nature's tune, we all take part.

So let us twirl beneath the trees,
And lose ourselves to twilight's breeze,
In every shadow, echoes stay,
The sprightly dance at end of day.

Whispers of the Wind Between Leaves

In rustling greens, a soft refrain,
The wind conveys a sweet domain,
Each whisper carries tales of old,
Of secrets wrapped in nature's fold.

Amongst the branches, breezes sweep,
They share the stories that they keep,
Of gentle rains and skies so blue,
Of every leaf, the dance anew.

The sun dips low, the shadows long,
The trees begin their evening song,
In every gust, a sigh is found,
A harmony, the world is bound.

With every breath, the secrets flow,
The whispers roam where few can go,
A language spoken soft and clear,
In every leaf, the world draws near.

So listen close to nature's heart,
In every breeze, we play our part,
For in the hush, we come alive,
With whispers of the wind, we thrive.

Honeyed Hues Beneath the Shade

In dappled light where shadows dance,
The world is bathed in golden chance,
Each honeyed hue a promise laid,
Beneath the branches' cool cascade.

The flowers bloom in vibrant grace,
Their colors blend, a warm embrace,
As laughter drifts on sunlit breeze,
In nature's soothing symphonies.

The sighing trees, they hold their shade,
In whispered tones, their secrets laid,
A refuge found from scorching sun,
Where moments pause and hearts are won.

Each fluttering leaf, a story spun,
In quiet places, joy is won,
With every breath, the time stands still,
In honeyed hues, the heart can fill.

So seek the shade where colors blend,
In tranquil nooks, our spirits mend,
For in this calm, we find our way,
With honeyed hues, we greet the day.

Whispers of the Enchanted Canopy

Beneath the leaves that softly sway,
Dreams are spun in shades of gray.
The twilight hums a gentle tune,
Awakening the night so soon.

In shadows deep, the secrets play,
Each flicker bright, a fleeting ray.
Nature's breath, a soothing sigh,
As starlit whispers drift on high.

Lost in the magic of this space,
I find my calm, a warm embrace.
The branches weave a tale untold,
Of countless wishes, dreams of gold.

Crickets serenade the night,
While fireflies dance, a wondrous sight.
The canopy, a sacred home,
Where hearts can wander, free to roam.

With every rustle, secrets shared,
In whispered breath, I know you're there.
Together in this twilight glow,
We'll trace the paths of long ago.

Luminous Laces in Twilight Glades

In glades where shadows start to blend,
Luminous threads above extend.
They stitch the sky with threads of light,
A tapestry through velvet night.

Dewdrops shimmer like tiny stars,
Adorning leaves, our nature's scars.
Every gust tells tales of fate,
While moonlight weaves a dance so great.

Winds whisper secrets, soft and low,
As gentle breezes come and go.
In this embrace, I lose my mind,
Among the wonders, sweetly kind.

Each moment captured, fleeting dreams,
Flow through the woods like silver streams.
The nighttime hugs the earth so tight,
While creatures stir, the world ignites.

With fragile hearts, the night we claim,
In luminous laces, no two the same.
Together woven, hand in hand,
In twilight glades, we make our stand.

Beneath the Gossamer Boughs

Beneath the boughs, so fine and light,
I wander deep into the night.
A gentle sway, the branches tease,
While shadows dance upon the breeze.

In gossamer veils, the world unfolds,
Tales of magic and warmth retold.
With every step, a whispered sound,
The heart of nature all around.

Moonlit pathways shape the view,
As softest murmurs weave anew.
Each rustling leaf, a note of grace,
Bids me pause in this sacred space.

In twilight's grasp, my spirit sighs,
A tapestry of dreams arise.
The cosmos cradles every star,
As dreams awaken, near and far.

With every heartbeat, life aligns,
In gossamer threads, our fate entwines.
Together here, with nature's breath,
We'll find our truth, defying death.

Secrets of the Hidden Grove

In hidden groves where silence reigns,
Echoes whisper through gentle veins.
A sacred hush holds ancient lore,
While time drifts softly to the floor.

Beneath the canopy's embrace,
Mossy carpets hide each trace.
The sun peeks through in golden beams,
Illuminating nature's dreams.

With every step, I find my way,
The earthy scents inviting stay.
Secrets linger in the air,
In every corner, everywhere.

The gentle brook sings its sweet song,
A symphony of right and wrong.
As shadows stretch, the dusk appears,
In a dance that calms all fears.

So here I stand, in awe, alone,
In hidden grove, a heart has grown.
With nature's mantle draped on me,
I cherish all that's meant to be.

Dappled Shadows and Dreaming Leaves

Beneath the ancient trees so wide,
Soft whispers of the breezes glide.
In dapples, shadows dance and play,
As sunlight weaves the dusk away.

Leaves flutter gently, dreams unfold,
Stories of the forest told.
In every rustle, secrets bloom,
A symphony in nature's room.

Through tangled boughs, the light streams gold,
A tapestry of green and bold.
In dreamy depths where shadows weave,
The heart finds rest, and hopes believe.

Ethereal Echoes in the Meadow

In meadows wide where lilies sway,
Ethereal echoes float and play.
Silken whispers kiss the air,
As daylight laughs without a care.

Each blossom sways, a soft embrace,
In every petal, love we trace.
From distant hills, the breezes call,
Their gentle songs enchant us all.

A dance of light, a fragrant tide,
In nature's arms, we seek to hide.
Where echoes linger, souls entwine,
In meadows rich, our hearts align.

The Lanterns of Unseen Worlds

In twilight's glow, the lanterns shine,
Casting light through realms divine.
They guide us to the hidden far,
Where dreams reside, a twinkling star.

With every flicker, stories pulse,
Of lost adventures, fate's convulse.
A bridge of light to worlds unknown,
In shadows deep, their glow is sown.

As night unfolds its velvet cloak,
The whispers rise, the lanterns spoke.
In unseen realms where magic swirls,
We wander 'neath their glowing pearls.

Threads of Magic in the Fiber of Night

In the twilight's hush, magic spins,
Threads of silver where dreaming begins.
Each star a note, a silent chime,
In the fabric of the night, sublime.

Woven whispers of ancient lore,
Guide us through the night's soft door.
Awakening hearts with a gentle light,
In shadows, we find our boundless flight.

The moon casts spells, a silken stream,
In the stillness, we dare to dream.
Threads of magic, a tapestry bright,
Knit together in the dark of night.

A Tapestry Woven with Moonlit Hues

In quiet night, the moonlight spills,
A silver thread on ancient hills.
Stars twinkle softly in endless skies,
Painting dreams where silence lies.

Each whisper of night, a secret told,
In patterns soft, in shadows bold.
The wind carries tales of love and fate,
Woven together, we patiently wait.

A tapestry rich, of heartstrings pulled,
Through memories vivid, forever ruled.
Embrace the beauty, let dreams ignite,
A dance of colors in gentle night.

With every glance, the world feels new,
In shades of night, the heart breaks through.
Underneath the sky, where wonders blend,
A timeless story that will not end.

The Flicker of Illusions in Eldritch Woods

In tangled paths where shadows creep,
The whispers of the woods run deep.
Moonlight dances on leaves so green,
Flickers of illusions, yet unseen.

Every rustle tells a tale unknown,
Echoes of laughter where secrets are sown.
Through twisted branches, visions play,
The heart wanders, lost in the fray.

A specter here, a shimmer there,
Chills the spine, fills the air.
Mysteries sway in the cool night breeze,
Enticing the dreamers among the trees.

In twilight's grasp, reality bends,
Where every story carefully wends.
A flicker of light, a sigh, a gleam,
In eldritch woods, lost in a dream.

Serenade of the Whispering Thicket

In the heart of the thicket, secrets sing,
Gentle voices of the spring.
Leaves rustle softly, a melodic tune,
Embraced by the glow of a silver moon.

Nightingales weave a symphony sweet,
Nature's orchestra, where lovers meet.
Echoes of harmony on soft, cool air,
A serenade whispered, a timeless affair.

Every branch sways in blissful dance,
Inviting hearts to take a chance.
With every note, the world holds still,
In the thicket's embrace, their dreams fulfill.

Stars listen close, as if to recall,
The rhythm of night, enchanting all.
In the serenade of the whispering thicket,
Magic lingers, an endless ticket.

Petals Cradled by the Moonlight

In a garden where silence blooms,
Petals sway softly under the moons.
Each drop of dew, a kiss of night,
Cradled in dreams, with pure delight.

Fragrant whispers fill the air,
A symphony woven from love's care.
Colors blend in softest embrace,
Nature's beauty, a fragile grace.

Moondrops shimmer on petals fair,
Lending each blossom a tender glare.
With every breeze, a story unfolds,
Of timeless love and memories bold.

As the stars watch over the sleeping blooms,
In moonlight's cradle, the heart resumes.
Petals slumber, bathed in light,
A peaceful promise through endless night.

Sylphs Charming the Quiet Woods

In the hush of the serene glade,
Sylphs dance where shadows fade.
Whispers weave through emerald leaves,
As twilight's magic softly weaves.

Glimmers of light dot the air,
Fleeting forms that flit with care.
Each murmur a gentle delight,
Guiding the night with their light.

Beneath the stars, they twirl and sway,
Guardian spirits at play.
With laughter like rippling streams,
They lull the world into dreams.

A symphony of rustling grace,
In their touch, the wild woods embrace.
Nature's secrets softly spoken,
In every spell, a bond unbroken.

Swaying through night's gentle bliss,
Sylphs bring magic that we miss.
In the quiet, they softly tread,
Where ancient realms stretch ahead.

Radiant Threads of a Forgotten Lore

In twilight's cloak, the stories lie,
Threads of lore in the sapphire sky.
Whispers of ages in each breeze,
A tapestry held by ancient trees.

Beneath the moon's soft silver glow,
The past unfolds in secrets slow.
Echoes linger in starlit haze,
Guiding hearts through shadowed days.

Each firefly blink, a memory bright,
Chasing the darkness, a fleeting light.
Legends born from the earth's deep core,
Revive the magic of days of yore.

Scribes of the winds, the nightingale sings,
Mortals tethered to forgotten things.
With every note, the past ignites,
Wrapping dreams in the quiet nights.

In silence, truths begin to gleam,
Radiant threads weave every dream.
Through nature's heart, they softly soar,
An echo of life in forgotten lore.

Glowing Vignettes of Nature's Breath

In the cradle of dawn's soft light,
Nature breathes with pure delight.
Petals unfurl, dew's jewels shine,
Whispering secrets of age-old time.

The forest hums a gentle tune,
As daylight dances, a fleeting boon.
Every rustle tells a tale,
Of fleeting moments, both vast and frail.

Birdsong weaves through the leafy maze,
In the warmth of the sun's embrace.
Fragments of life, a vivid brush,
With colors that shimmer, spark, and rush.

The brook babbles in playful glee,
Reflecting wonders for all to see.
Glowing vignettes framed by the day,
Nature's art in intricate play.

As twilight drapes in shades of deep,
Life's fleeting moments we shall keep.
In the hush of night, we find our tether,
To glowing vignettes that bind us together.

Swaying Hearts in Sylvan Groves

In the heart of the sylvan glades,
Swaying hearts find whispered serenades.
Nature cradles every soul,
In her embrace, we become whole.

Beneath the arches of ancient trees,
Love takes flight on the gentle breeze.
With every rustle, whispers bloom,
Filling the air with sweet perfume.

The dance of shadows, light entwined,
In this haven, freedom we find.
Cascading leaves in twilight's glow,
A rhythm as soft as the river's flow.

Every glance, a quiet vow,
In the woods, time pauses now.
A symphony of hearts at play,
Drawing closer as night turns to day.

Bonds of love in nature's weave,
Swaying gently, we believe.
In sylvan groves, we rediscover,
The beauty of life, shared with each other.

The Enigma of the Woodland Spirits

In the hush of trees, whispers call,
Mysteries dance with shadows tall.
Moonlight weaves through branches tight,
Guarding secrets of the night.

Elusive forms, they flit and sway,
Fleeting visions in the gray.
A rustle here, a glance so rare,
They vanish into thin, cool air.

Eyes like embers, bright and keen,
Life's enigma, lost, unseen.
Their laughter echoes, soft and clear,
Drawing us near, yet far, they veer.

Under boughs where silence reigns,
Magic pulses through the veins.
In glades where sunlight seldom spills,
The woodland spirits weave their thrills.

So wander softly, tread with care,
For their presence lingers there.
In every rustle, breeze, and sigh,
The woodland spirits dance and fly.

Sprites and Shadows in Twilight's Hold

As daylight fades, shadows creep,
In twilight's veil, secrets keep.
Sprites emerge with laughter light,
Playing games in fading sight.

The colors blend, a gentle art,
Whispers flutter, hearts to part.
In the gloaming, joy takes flight,
A waltz of shadows, pure delight.

Beneath the stars, they spin and twine,
Threading dreams with wishes fine.
In every sparkle, hopes reborn,
From the dusk till the early morn.

The air is thick with soft embrace,
In twilight's glow, a hidden place.
Where sprites convene, a fest divine,
An ephemeral dance by design.

So gaze upon the dusking skies,
Where magic lingers, never dies.
In shadows deep, life's mirth unfolds,
Sprites and shadows in twilight's hold.

Glimmers of Hope Among the Greenery

Beneath the leaves, a light does beam,
A promise wrapped in emerald dream.
Hope arises with each gentle breeze,
Whispers of life among the trees.

Dew-kissed petals, soft and bright,
Glimmers dance in morning light.
Nature's canvas, bold and free,
Colors bloom with harmony.

In every nook, a tale unfolds,
The warmth of sunshine, secrets told.
Little treasures in every glade,
A tapestry of life is laid.

From tangled roots to soaring skies,
Glimmers of hope will always rise.
In every shadow, in every sigh,
The heart finds wings, and soars on high.

So walk with wonder, take it slow,
Among the greenery, let love grow.
For glimmers of hope, forever shine,
In the heart of nature, pure and divine.

Serendipity Among the Blossomed Dreams

In gardens bright where daybeams play,
Serendipity finds her way.
Among the blooms, sweet scents arise,
Whispers of joy greet the skies.

Petals flutter, hearts rejoice,
Nature sings, a vibrant voice.
In every breeze that brushes past,
Moments of magic, too lovely, too fast.

Among the blossoms, dreams alight,
Softly glowing, pure and bright.
A dance of possibilities unfolds,
A tapestry of stories told.

Each fragrant step, a step toward grace,
In the bloom of life, we find our place.
As colors mingle, life's sweet schemes,
Find serendipity in our dreams.

So wander through this wondrous scene,
In every flower, find the serene.
For in the garden, life's dreams redeem,
Serendipity among the blossomed dreams.

Lanterns of Light on Mossy Paths

Amidst the trees, soft glow does gleam,
Mossy paths weave through a dream.
Whispers of night, gentle and bright,
Guiding the wanderers with delight.

Each lantern sways with a sigh,
Illuminating secrets that lie,
In the still air, magic unfolds,
Stories of old, quietly told.

Crickets serenade the weary soul,
As shadows dance, making us whole.
Lanterns flicker, a comforting sight,
Leading us home through the night.

The forest breathes, alive with cheer,
In every twinkle, love draws near.
Moss-clad stones, in silence they bask,
In twilight's arms, all dreams unmask.

So step with care on this emerald trail,
Where lanterns whisper and never pale.
In the embrace of the night, we bring,
The light of our hearts, the joy we sing.

Delicate Murmurs of Celestial Beings

In the realm where stardust flows,
Celestial whispers softly compose.
Murmurs of light from worlds afar,
Guiding our hearts like a shooting star.

Ethereal beings dance in the skies,
With grace unbound, they rise and sigh.
Each twinkle a tale from ages past,
In the silence, their magic is cast.

Listening close, we hear the song,
Of cosmic harmony, pure and strong.
Delicate notes that weave and blend,
A symphony sweet that never ends.

Glimmers of hope in every stroke,
Woven with dreams that gently woke.
In the vastness, we find our place,
Embraced by love, wrapped in grace.

As night descends, the whispers grow,
A tapestry of stars on the flow.
In the stillness, we feel their light,
Delicate murmurs, a guiding sight.

Ethereal Sights Beneath the Emerald Veil

Beneath the canopy, shadows play,
In the emerald veil, dreams gently sway.
Ethereal sights that dazzle the mind,
Secrets of nature, beautifully kind.

Whispers of leaves in a gentle breeze,
Murmurs of magic that put us at ease.
Glimmers of dawn break through the green,
A world reborn, serene and pristine.

In every rustle, stories emerge,
From ancient roots, the past can surge.
Beneath the sky, the wonders ignite,
In ethereal dances, pure delight.

Soft petals shimmer, like stars in the night,
Each flower a promise, glowing bright.
In this tranquil realm, our spirits unfurl,
Embraced by the wonders of a magical world.

So linger awhile in this mystic glade,
Where time fades gently, memories made.
In nature's arms, we find our way,
Ethereal sights guide us each day.

Candles of Fairytale Light

In the heart of the woods, soft sparks arise,
Candles of dreams dance beneath the skies.
Flickering flames, a warm embrace,
Casting shadows with a tender grace.

Each glow tells tales of love and delight,
In fairytale realms, so charmingly bright.
Whispers of wishes, wishes so sweet,
Brought to life with each flicker and beat.

The night unveils stories from yore,
Adventures that linger, forevermore.
With every candle, our hopes take flight,
Illuminating paths in the hush of night.

In gardens of wonder, we pause and reflect,
On memories made, the joys we collect.
Candles aglow like stars in the dark,
Filling our hearts with a magical spark.

So let us wander where the fairytales grow,
Under the candles' gentle glow.
In the warmth of their light, dreams come alive,
A world full of wonder, where spirits thrive.

Wisps of Wonder Among the Leaves

In the cradle of the green, it whispers,
Secrets carried on the breeze,
Rustling dreams through branches sway,
Nature's hymn, a gentle tease.

Flashes of light in dappled shade,
Dancing softly, fleeting show,
Voices of the woodlands call,
Echoes of long tales below.

A flicker here, a shimmer there,
Golden glints on emerald floor,
Where shadows meld in quiet peace,
And wonder opens every door.

Leaves embrace the midday sun,
Kissed by warmth, adorned in grace,
Whispers linger ever near,
With every rustle, time's embrace.

A realm where magic intertwines,
Each glance a spark of sweet delight,
With wisps of wonder we explore,
Among the leaves, a wondrous sight.

Veils of Light in the Forest's Embrace

Veils of mist weave through the trees,
Soft and silent, they descend,
Caressing bark and fern alike,
In this sanctuary blend.

Sunlight filters through the boughs,
Painting trails of golden hue,
Nature's canvas comes alive,
With every glance, a world anew.

Whispers float on gentle winds,
Carried softly from afar,
Where shadows play and secrets lie,
Beneath the watchful evening star.

Every glimmer, every glow,
Tells a tale from days of yore,
In this abode where spirits dwell,
And dreams take flight forevermore.

Veils of light, a soft embrace,
Wrap the heart in nature's grace,
In a world where time stands still,
The forest's magic finds its place.

The Song of Fern Fronds and Stardust

Underneath the canopy,
A symphony of rust and green,
Fern fronds sway with whispered tunes,
In a world both rich and serene.

Cradled in the evening glow,
Stardust lingers in the air,
Echoing the night's crisp call,
With secrets fraught yet oh so rare.

Moonlight dances on each leaf,
Casting shadows soft and bright,
As nature holds its breath in awe,
Beneath the shroud of silver night.

The song of fronds, a sweet refrain,
Calls to hearts both wild and free,
In this sanctuary of dreams,
A timeless bond with earth and sea.

With every note, new worlds arise,
In harmony, the cosmos sings,
The dance of life, an endless flow,
Where starlight dreams and magic springs.

Mystical Fragments of Celestial Bloom

In the stillness of the night,
When shadows stretch and stars appear,
Fragments of dreams scatter wide,
Celestial blooms in cosmic sphere.

Whirls of color paint the sky,
A tapestry of radiant light,
Each blossom holds a whisper true,
Of distant worlds and endless flight.

Galaxies twirl in silent grace,
While time unfurls its ancient tale,
Guiding us through cosmic paths,
As constellations softly sail.

A dance of petals, bright and bold,
Awakening hearts to explore,
Mysteries where stardust sings,
Of dreams that linger evermore.

In the magic of night's embrace,
Fragments spark a newfound bloom,
Celestial whispers come alive,
In this enchanting, endless room.

Illusions in the Whispering Boughs

In twilight's glow, shadows dance light,
Leaves murmur secrets, fading from sight.
Whispers hang low in the still, cool air,
Echoing dreams that linger with care.

Moonlit paths lead to enchanting dreams,
Where nothing is ever quite as it seems.
The branches sway with a subtle tease,
Inviting wishes on the gentle breeze.

Amidst the night's hush, a soft voice calls,
Telling stories of love beneath the thralls.
Illusions weave through the tangled boughs,
Painting the night with unspoken vows.

In the heart of dusk, wonder aligns,
A dance of magic where fate intertwines.
Through the curtain of branches, a glimpse ignites,
A world awash in eternal delights.

As daylight fades and the stars ignite,
Embrace the enchantment of the night.
In illusions found through the whispering trees,
Life unfolds gently, just like the leaves.

The Spellbound Forest's Call

Deep in the woods where the old oaks sigh,
Magic lingers under the starlit sky.
Moss carpets ground, soft as a dream,
Holding secrets untold in a silver gleam.

The wind carries songs from ages past,
Tales of enchantment, shadows cast.
Every fern and flower tells a story,
Wrapped in splendor, cloaked in glory.

A hush falls softly, the world holds its breath,
In the realm where whispers flirt with death.
Nature's chorus in a gentle thrall,
Invites the weary to heed the call.

Moonbeams wander through branches wide,
Inviting souls on a magical ride.
The forest beckons with its embrace,
Offering solace and a sacred space.

With every step in this spellbound glade,
Lose your doubts in the twilight shade.
Let the echoes guide, let your spirit soar,
For the forest awaits with wonders in store.

Nightfall in a Haven of Whispers

As dusk descends, the world softly fades,
And quiet secrets in the shadows cascade.
Stars blink awake in the velvet sky,
While softly the night starts to sigh.

The air is thick with unspoken dreams,
Where wishes are born amidst silvery streams.
In this haven, where shadows convene,
Echoes of laughter float softly, unseen.

Whispers of breezes, light as a sigh,
Dancing through branches, like a secret reply.
Nightfall reveals what daylight won't show,
The heart of the world in a gentle glow.

In the stillness, the moon takes her throne,
Illuminating paths that lead us home.
Each step a promise, each glance a vow,
To treasure the whispers that guide us now.

So linger a moment in this mystic space,
Where dreams intertwine, and time slows its pace.
For in night's embrace, magic sweetly flows,
In a haven of whispers where love only grows.

Fables in the Fern-Cloaked Nook

In a hidden nook where fables bloom,
Fern leaves cradle the whispers of gloom.
Stories entangle in the misty air,
Anticipated wonder woven with care.

Sunlight dapples through a leafy dome,
While tales of old find purpose and home.
Eager hearts listen as shadows unfold,
Every flicker of light shares a story told.

In this tranquil space, magic takes flight,
Imagination dances with sheer delight.
Every rustle, a clue to the past,
Inviting the dreamers, safe and steadfast.

Legends are painted in silken hues,
Crafting a world with the softest muse.
In a fern-cloaked nook where dreams transcend,
Fables linger softly, in silence, they blend.

So wander these paths where wonders ignite,
In the cradle of foliage that shimmers with light.
Celebrate stories that beckon and call,
In the heart of the woods, there's magic for all.

The Green Enclave of Forgotten Songs

In shadows deep where whispers dwell,
The breeze recalls a distant swell.
Old melodies entwined with leaves,
In silence, nature softly weaves.

Each note a tale of days gone by,
Underneath a cerulean sky.
The songs of old, now soft and faint,
In every rustle, a sweet complaint.

Through tangled roots and vibrant ferns,
A harmony that softly churns.
The echoes merge with twilight's glow,
In secret corners, tales still flow.

Lost voices linger in the air,
A serenade of love and care.
They linger here, within the shade,
In every gust, their presence made.

So join the dance of leaf and light,
In this enclave, pure delight.
For every song once softly sung,
Lives on, forever young.

The Crooning of the Elder Trees

Beneath the boughs of ancient giants,
A symphony of soft defiance.
Their gnarled branches hold the past,
In crooning tones that ever last.

Through timeworn bark, the stories flow,
Of seasons passed and seeds that grow.
The whispers of the winds they share,
A timeless tune that fills the air.

With roots entwined in earth's embrace,
They sing of age and slow grace.
Each rustle a harmonic sigh,
In quiet moments when spirits fly.

Their leafy crowns, a choir grand,
Creating music across the land.
The crooning echoes deep and wide,
In their strong arms, we softly bide.

When night descends and shadows creep,
They serenade the world to sleep.
In every breeze, a lullaby,
The elder trees, they never die.

Twilight's Garden of Mystical Spirits

In twilight's hush, where shadows blend,
A garden waits, where secrets mend.
With petals soft and colors bright,
The spirits stir and take to flight.

They dance upon the evening dew,
With laughter light, a playful crew.
The flowers bloom, their whispers sweet,
In twilight's glow, our hearts they greet.

Each shimmer in the twilight air,
A promise made, a silent prayer.
The spirits weave their gentle art,
In every bloom, there beats a heart.

Moonlight beckons, a silver thread,
Through petaled dreams, the night is spread.
In twilight's garden, time stands still,
With every breeze, a gentle thrill.

So wander deep where silence sings,
Amongst the blooms, where magic clings.
For here in this enchanted space,
The mystical, we dare embrace.

Secrets Cradled by Timeworn Boughs

In branches bent with age and care,
Secrets sleep in the crisp night air.
Timeworn boughs, they guard the dreams,
Whispers hidden in gentle streams.

The stories etched in every ring,
Dance on the winds as the robins sing.
From verdant roots to tips of gold,
Legendary tales of the brave and bold.

In silent nights, the owls declare,
The hidden lore of earth laid bare.
With every rustle of their leaves,
A timeless truth the forest heaves.

Through shadows deep, the path is clear,
For those who dare, the heart will steer.
In timeworn boughs, their secrets dwell,
A tapestry of life to tell.

So linger here, where moments pause,
And listen close, respect their cause.
For in the woods, both wild and free,
Lie whispers of eternity.

Gossamer Dreams in the Forest Shade

Whispers of leaves dance in the breeze,
Misty tendrils weave through the trees.
Gossamer veils in twilight's embrace,
Nature's secrets in a hidden place.

Moonlight glimmers on the forest floor,
Echoes of magic, soft shadows soar.
Crickets serenade the night sky's jam,
While fireflies twinkle, a shimmering dram.

The brook sings softly, a lullaby sweet,
In the heart of the woods, where dreams meet.
Elusive creatures flit out of sight,
Merging with darkness, embracing the night.

Beneath ancient boughs, stories unfold,
Of timeless wonders and legends old.
Each rustle and murmur a tale to share,
In gossamer dreams, we float in the air.

In the embrace of the night's gentle arms,
We find solace in nature's charms.
Lost in the magic, we quietly sigh,
As the forest breathes softly, and the stars fly high.

The Dappled Light of Otherworlds

Sunbeams filter through leaves of green,
Creating patterns in places unseen.
Dappled light spills across the glade,
Guiding lost souls through the enchanting shade.

In this realm where shadows play,
The whispers of spirits linger and sway.
Every flicker reveals tales untold,
Of ancient magic and dreams of old.

Petals glisten with dew like stars,
The air alive with their fragrant memoirs.
A soft breeze carries melodies sweet,
Inviting the wanderer to feel the beat.

Mystic paths weave through underbrush tight,
Leading us deeper into the light.
With each step, the whirl of the past
Grows stronger, like shadows that never last.

Boundless wonders unfold as we roam,
In this dance of the light, we find our home.
The dappled glow holds secrets so bright,
In this otherworld, our spirits take flight.

A Glimpse into Fae Realms

Beneath the oak, where the wildflowers grow,
The fae weave spells in the twilight glow.
A fleeting glimpse of wings, soft and light,
As laughter echoes in the coming night.

Moonlit dances on petals in bloom,
Magic drifts softly, dispelling the gloom.
Whispers of wishes ride on the breeze,
Awakening dreams among ancient trees.

Mirth and mischief under the stars,
The fae gather close, sharing their bars.
With sparkling eyes and delight in their song,
They call to the heart where the lost souls belong.

In twilight's embrace, they revel and play,
With gossamer threads weaving night into day.
A glimpse of their world, so enchanting and bright,
In the cradle of shadows, the magic ignites.

Yet just as the dawn begins to unfold,
They vanish like dreams, elusive and bold.
But the essence remains, lingering near,
In the hush of the forest, we hold them dear.

Shadows Waltzing with Sunlight

Morning breaks with a gentle sigh,
Shadows dance where daylight draws nigh.
In a rhythm born from whispers so sweet,
Sunlight and shadows, a delicate feat.

Leaves tremble softly, swaying with grace,
While the sun kisses earth with a warm embrace.
In this ballet of light, stories unfold,
Of fleeting moments, both quiet and bold.

An endless waltz on the forest floor,
Each step echoing tales of yore.
As patterns play hide-and-seek on the ground,
Nature's symphony sings without a sound.

The brook joins in, a soft lilting tune,
Awakening dreams in the light of the moon.
The dance of the day and the night intertwines,
Creating a tapestry where magic aligns.

As dusk descends, the shadows grow deep,
The sunlight retreats, but the magic won't sleep.
In the heart of the forest where spirits reside,
Shadows waltzing with sunlight, forever abide.

Quicksilver Flights of Fairy Chimes

In twilight's grace, the fairies sigh,
With whispers soft, they dance and fly.
Their silver wings in moonlight gleam,
A world enchanted, like a dream.

Through wooded glades and blooming flowers,
They weave their magic, greet the hours.
A symphony of soft delight,
In every flicker of the night.

The air is filled with laughter's ring,
As chimes of joy the fairies bring.
Each note a promise, sweet and bright,
In myriad forms, they take their flight.

Above the brook where shadows play,
They dart like beads of light all day.
With painted skies and swirling air,
Each moment holds a magic rare.

So close your eyes, let senses soar,
And feel the pulse of ancient lore.
For in their flight, we find the song,
A timeless dance where we belong.

A Reverie Among the Faery Boughs

In dappled light where shadows blend,
The faeries weave, their dreams suspend.
Upon the boughs, where silence hums,
A world of wonder gently comes.

With whispers soft, they brew the night,
With every breath, their hearts take flight.
From blooms of gold to starlit skies,
The magic swirls, it never dies.

They gather near the silver stream,
Where moonlight spills and starlight beams.
Each gentle laugh, a spark ignites,
In every tale, the spirit unites.

A glimmer here, a shimmer there,
Among the boughs, no worries care.
Just laughter mingling in the air,
In nature's heart, so sweet and rare.

Close your eyes and let them show,
The secrets hidden down below.
In reveries of joy and song,
Among the faery boughs, belong.

The Lair of Enchanted Echoes

In caverns deep where shadows play,
The echoes call from far away.
With whispered tones, they stir the night,
A haunting song, a flickering light.

Through twisted roots and ancient stone,
The spirits dwell, no longer lone.
With tales of yore and dreams they keep,
The echo's lull will sing us to sleep.

Each murmur speaks of fables lost,
Of journeys made, of bridges crossed.
The heartbeats of the earth combine,
In every sound, a spark divine.

In silver mists, the secrets flow,
As time transcends, we come to know.
The lair awaits, where shadows creep,
Into the depths, our spirits leap.

So linger here, let echoes roam,
You'll find a sense that feels like home.
For in the depths of every sigh,
The enchanted echoes never die.

Glimpses of Twilight's Embrace

When day surrenders to the night,
A canvas brushed with soft twilight.
In hues of purple, blue, and gold,
The breath of secrets yet untold.

Through whispers of the cooling breeze,
The tales of stars begin to tease.
Each glimmer holds a wish anew,
A glimpse of what the heart holds true.

With every sigh, the shadows dance,
Inviting dreams to take their chance.
Where twinkling lights, like fireflies,
Illuminate the darkened skies.

In twilight's cloak, we feel the pull,
A magic realm, enchanting, full.
With open hearts, and eyes aglow,
We touch the stars, let dreams bestow.

So linger long, in twilight's grace,
Embrace the night, its soft embrace.
For in the quiet, beauty gleams,
And whispers softly, fuel our dreams.

Moonlit Paths of Fae Wonder

Underneath the silver glow,
Whispers float like dreams aglow.
Fae dance softly, shadows gleam,
In a realm where lost hearts scheme.

Twinkling stardust trails behind,
Guiding all who seek to find.
Elven laughter, soft and rare,
Winding through the fragrant air.

Beckoning with every breeze,
Mysteries among the trees.
Moonlit paths where secrets lie,
Invite wanderers to fly.

Glimmers radiate from stones,
Heartbeats echo with soft tones.
Daring souls that venture near,
Meet enchantments, cast away fear.

In the glow, courage will bloom,
Chasing away the creeping gloom.
Magic threads in twilight's hour,
Binding peace with gentle power.

Tales from the Eldritch Shade

In shadows deep, where secrets crawl,
Ancient whispers softly call.
Eldritch tales woven with dread,
Breathe life to dreams, both lost and dead.

Rustling leaves hide stories old,
In every crack, a secret told.
Nighttime gardens thrum and hum,
Cardinal truths that strain to come.

Cloaked in silence, specters creep,
Haunting echoes from the deep.
Twisted roots and gnarled trees,
Guard the essence of the breeze.

Beneath the moon's all-seeing eye,
Graphics of tales that never die.
Spirits roam with a gentle grace,
Concealing truths in a shadowed space.

Ink of night spills onto ground,
Scribing destinies that astound.
With every tale that tempts the shade,
Lies a beauty not afraid.

A Symphony of Glowing Through the Leaves

Moonbeams play on emerald boughs,
Nature's music, all things rouse.
A symphony whispers on the wind,
Blossoms sway, melodies pinned.

Dancing leaves in twilight's grace,
Curling soft in sweet embrace.
Each note sings of life anew,
Painting skies in vibrant hue.

Crickets chirp a calming tune,
While fireflies flicker, bright as June.
An orchestra of fading light,
Fills the heart with pure delight.

As the stars above take flight,
Feel the magic twinkling bright.
In harmony, all things unite,
Threads of beauty in the night.

Gather 'round, let worries cease,
Join the song of nature's peace.
In the glow, we lose our fears,
A symphony that lasts for years.

Blossoms of Mystique in the Faery Glen

Beneath the bowers, soft and fair,
Mystic blooms release sweet air.
Petals whisper tales untold,
In gardens where the secrets unfold.

Moonlit rays on fragile skin,
Embodied dance, where dreams begin.
Faery glen, enchanting sight,
Where wonders live and hearts take flight.

Roses blush in shades of gold,
Held in silence, nature's fold.
Fragrant breezes gently play,
Guiding hearts along their way.

Rippling streams with laughter flow,
Mirror images, soft and slow.
In this realm, where magic's spun,
Life and dreams forever run.

Childlike wonder blooms anew,
In the glen, where wishes brew.
Whispers linger on the air,
In these blossoms, magic's there.

Echoing Laughter of Woodlands Fairies

In the dappled light they play,
Chasing shadows, night and day.
Laughter rings through vale and glen,
Whispers soft like summer's den.

Dancing under ancient trees,
With the rustling of the leaves.
Joyful songs in evening's glow,
Echoes of the dreams they sow.

Mirthful sprites in twilight's embrace,
Sprinkling stardust, leaving trace.
Glimmers of magic in the air,
A tapestry of dreams to share.

Beneath the moon's soft silver beam,
They weave together joy and dream.
Forever bound by nature's art,
In woodlands where their laughter starts.

So if you wander through the glade,
And hear their laughter, do not fade.
Join the dance, become a part,
Of woodlands fairies, heart to heart.

Spirits of the Misty Grove

In the mist where shadows creep,
Spirits guard the secrets deep.
With a sigh, they softly glide,
Through the trees, they do reside.

Glimmering orbs in twilight fade,
Guiding lost souls, unafraid.
Bound by love and ancient lore,
They beckon gently to the shore.

Whispers echo, soft and low,
Carried by the cool night's flow.
A dance beneath the starry light,
Spirits twirl, with pure delight.

In the heart of the groves so old,
Stories of their bravery told.
Here in this enchanted place,
They find solace, peace, and grace.

So tread lightly through the mist,
And catch the magic on your wrist.
For in the grove where spirits roam,
You may find a kindred home.

Leafy Whispers and Glittering Paths

Through the branches, secrets shared,
With each rustle, hearts laid bare.
Leafy whispers in the breeze,
Lifting dreams high in the trees.

Glittering paths through emerald hills,
Where the quiet magic thrills.
Nature's song, a symphony,
Calling forth the wild and free.

Dappled sunlight, golden hue,
Every moment feels so new.
Join the dance of earth and sky,
Wander where the fairies fly.

Tap your feet upon the ground,
Listen closely to the sound.
Every leaf a tale to tell,
Of ancient woods where spirits dwell.

With each turn, a story fades,
In the charm of leafy glades.
So journey forth with heart and mind,
And leave the world of man behind.

A Realm of Verdant Fantasies

In a realm where dreams take flight,
Verdant visions spark the night.
Whispers dance on breezes light,
Creating magic out of sight.

Echoes of a laughter sweet,
Mingle with the woodland's beat.
Every flower holds a spark,
In this realm, no place is dark.

Where the ferns and grasses sway,
Time stands still, night and day.
Gentle creatures softly roam,
In this world, they find their home.

Butterflies with wings like dreams,
Fluttering through golden beams.
Painted skies of hues so bright,
Crafting wonder, pure delight.

So close your eyes and take a leap,
Into the fantasies you keep.
In fresh green, your spirit free,
Feel the magic, come and be.

The Hidden Lair of Arcane Wonders

In shadows deep where secrets sleep,
The whispers of the night do creep.
A glimmer spark amidst the gloom,
Awakens hearts, dispels the doom.

Forgotten paths of ancient lore,
Unlocking mysteries at the core.
With flickering lights of emerald hue,
The hidden lair beckons you.

Each tome reveals a sacred tale,
Of wistful dreams that dared to sail.
Through corridors where echoes blend,
Magic stirs, around the bend.

A flick of wand, a silent chant,
In this realm where phantoms slant.
The air is thick with vibrant sights,
A dance of spells and starry nights.

Within the lair, your heart may race,
For here lies time's enchanting face.
From dust and whispers, artful fates,
Are stitched in dreams, at destiny's gates.

Petals of Illumination

In gardens bright where colors play,
Petals whisper of the day.
They dance beneath the sun's warm gaze,
In a vibrant ballet, lost in a haze.

Each bloom a story, soft and sweet,
A tapestry where life's threads meet.
Colors mix like laughter shared,
In fragrant air, hearts are bared.

From crimson blush to azure sky,
Every petal breathes a sigh.
A gentle breeze, a lover's tune,
As nature hums a lovely rune.

With dew-kissed dawn, the world awakes,
Each petal shimmered, the soul it shakes.
A symphony of light unfurls,
In this realm where magic swirls.

Beneath the petals, secrets lie,
In the heart of each flower, a sigh.
Illumination in every hue,
Guiding lost souls to something new.

Beneath the Canopy of Whimsy

Underneath the leafy boughs,
Whispers spin and nature bows.
A realm of laughter, bright and bold,
Where dreams and wonders unfold.

With every step, a breathless thrill,
Through vibrant air, the spirits spill.
Playful light in shadows cast,
A glimpse of futures, echoes past.

Here, the flowers wear their smiles,
While time slumbers in carefree miles.
Mischief danced with fairy lights,
As day slips into starry nights.

Underneath the giggles high,
Beneath the arch of cotton sky.
A world where whimsy reigns supreme,
Each moment blooming like a dream.

The trees may sigh, the breezes tease,
As laughter floats upon the breeze.
Under this canopy, hearts awake,
For joy is real, make no mistake.

Tapestries Woven with Stardust

In nights adorned with velvet skies,
Stardust weaves through silent sighs.
Tapestries of dreams unveiled,
In cosmic wonders, we have sailed.

Threads of silver, whispers glow,
In the fabric of the night's soft flow.
Each twinkle holds a fabled tale,
As wishes drift on moonlit trails.

We gather stardust in our hands,
Creating magic where life stands.
With every weave, the past entwines,
In patterns bright, our fate aligns.

Through every stitch, a heartbeat found,
In the quiet night, love's profound.
For in the cosmos, we are one,
Woven tight till the night is done.

Beneath the stars, let spirits soar,
As dreams weave tales forevermore.
In every shimmer, a promise stays,
In tapestries that time delays.